◄ NATIVE AMERICAN PEOPLE ►

THE CHOCTAW

by Victoria Sherrow

Illustrated by Richard Smolinski

ROURKE PUBLICATIONS, INC.

VERO BEACH, FLORIDA 32964

CONTENTS

Library of Congress Cataloging-in-Publication Data

Sherrow, Victoria.
    The Choctaw / by Victoria Sherrow : illustrated by Richard Smolinksi.
      p.   cm. — (Native American people)
    Includes index.
    Summary: Discusses the history and culture of the Choctaw.
    ISBN 0-86625-602-4
    1. Choctaw Indians—History—Juvenile literature.
2. Choctaw Indians—Social life and customs—Juvenile literature. [1. Choctaw Indians. 2. Indians of North America—Southern States.]
I. Smolinski, Dick, ill. II. Title. III. Series.
E99.C8S57 1997
973'.04973—dc21   97-9628
                                     CIP
                                       AC

Introduction

For many years, archaeologists—and other people who study early Native American cultures—believed that the first humans to live in the Americas arrived in Alaska from Siberia between 11,000 and 12,000 years ago. Stone spear points and other artifacts dating to that time were discovered in many parts of the Americas.

The first Americans probably arrived by way of a vast bridge of land between Siberia and Alaska. The land link emerged from the sea when Ice Age glaciers lowered the level of the world's oceans.

The first migration across the bridge was most likely an accident. It appears that bands of hunters from Asia followed herds of mammoths, giant bison, and other Ice Age game that roamed the 1,000-mile-wide bridge. Over a long time—perhaps thousands of years—some of the hunters arrived in Alaska.

Many scholars now suggest that the first Americans may have arrived in North America as early as 30,000 or even 50,000 years ago. Some of these early Americans may not have crossed the bridge to the New World. They may have arrived by boat, working their way down the west coasts of North America and South America.

In support of this theory, scientists who study language or genetics (the study of the inherited similarities and differences found in living things) believe that there may have been many migrations of peoples over the bridge to North America. There are about 200 different Native American languages, which vary greatly. In addition to speaking different languages, groups of Native Americans can look as physically different as, for example, Italians and Swedes. These facts lead some scientists to suspect that multiple migrations started in different parts of Asia. If this is true, then Native Americans descend not from one people, but from many.

After they arrived in Alaska, different groups of early Native Americans fanned out over North America and South America. They inhabited almost every corner of these two continents, from the shores of the Arctic Ocean in the north to Tierra del Fuego, at the southern tip of South America. Over this immense area, there were many different environments, which changed with the passage of time. The lifestyles of early Americans adapted to these environments and changed with them.

In what is now Mexico, some Native Americans built great cities and developed agriculture. Farming spread north. So did the concentration of people in large communities, which was the result of successful farming. In other regions of the Americas, agriculture was not as important. Wild animals and plants were the main sources of food for native hunters and gatherers.

Agriculture was very important to the 75 or so different tribes of Native Americans who settled in the southeastern part of the United States. The fertile soil and sunny climate enabled them to raise crops and build permanent villages.

One of the largest and most powerful tribes was the Choctaw. It was one of what became known as the Five Civilized Tribes, which also included the Cherokee, Creek, Seminole, and Chickasaw.

The Choctaw lived in present-day east-central Mississippi. They occupied about 26 million acres of rich land, dotted with pine forests and rivers. To the southwest lived the Natchez Indians, in what is now Louisiana. Northwest of the Choctaw were the Quapaw of present-day Arkansas.

Origins of the Choctaw

Scientists believe that Native Americans have lived in the southeastern United States for at least 10,000 years. The Choctaw people probably had the same ancestors as the Chickasaw tribe, who lived in present-day northern Mississippi and Alabama. According to an old legend, the ancestors of the Chickasaw and Choctaw once lived farther to the west. Led by two brothers, Chicsa and Chacta, they moved east, looking for the best place to settle down. The brothers quarreled, and Chicsa took his people north, to the place now called Tennessee. The other brother, named Chacta, led his group farther south. They became the Choctaw people.

The two tribes have similar languages, which developed from the Muskogean family of Native American languages. The Muskogean languages

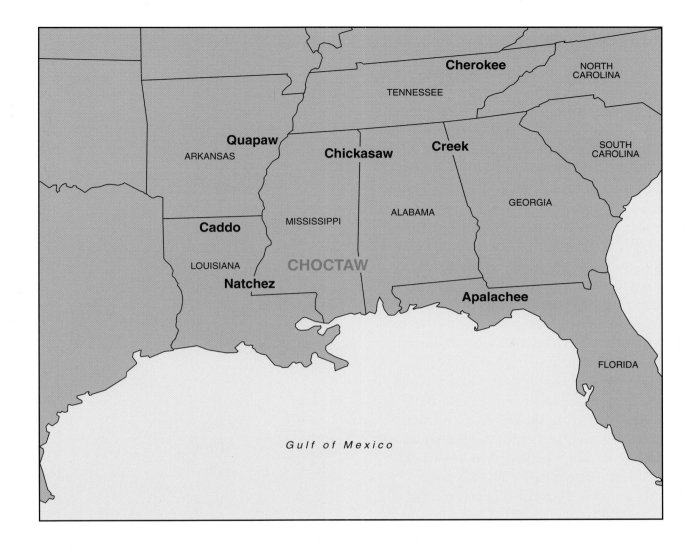

Gulf of Mexico

are in turn part of a larger group, called "Gulf languages." The name *Choctaw* comes from the Creek word, *chate*, which means "red."

Thousands of years ago, the Choctaw were nomadic. They moved about, hunting and fishing for their food and gathering wild plants. Hunters made stone spearheads to kill game, which was mainly deer.

Around the year A.D. 900, the Choctaw learned how to grow corn, their first and principal crop. Corn was the main food in Central America, where people had learned to grow it from a wild plant. Native Americans found many uses for fresh corn, and they stored it in the form of grain and meal. Dependable harvests enabled the Choctaw to build settled communities and to develop a rich culture.

The Choctaw traded with other southeastern tribes. The tribes developed a language for trading based on Choctaw words. Among other things, they traded the pelts of bears and beavers, buffalo robes, bear oil, seashells, freshwater pearls, and copper. The Choctaw sometimes had some extra corn or other crops to trade. They were known as a thrifty people.

Daily Life

The Choctaw located their villages near rivers, streams, or other good sources of water. Villages tended to be large, with some holding 200 or 300 homes. Walls and moats were built around the village to keep out enemies. Many outdoor ceremonies and rituals took place in the village square, where there were also tribal buildings for public use.

Good raw materials were available for construction. The Choctaw made their homes from wood, thatch, bark, and reeds, such as cane. Families usually owned two dwellings. The summer home held separate areas for cooking and for sleeping and sitting. Walls made from woven mats had holes for letting in fresh air. Additional woven mats that hung above these holes could be lowered to cover the holes and keep the homes warmer.

To build their winter homes, the Choctaw wove saplings together. They packed a mixture of grass and clay between the cracks in the walls to keep out bad weather. Roofs were made out of thatch. On cold nights, the Choctaw poured water over hot stones inside their homes in order to create steam heat.

Choctaw homes were furnished simply. People slept on beds made from poles that were covered with mats and animal skins or furs. Other belongings kept in the house included clothing, pots and eating utensils, tools and weapons. The Choctaw homes and household goods were considered the property of the women.

A mother and daughter prepare food outside of their traditional thatched house.

Family Life

A Choctaw family consisted of a mother, father, and children. Everyone had special roles and duties. Besides working to sustain their own families, the Choctaw also spent time on work that helped the whole village, such as cultivating the communal vegetable plot.

Men could be farmers, warriors, fishermen, traders, priests, medicine men, and tribal leaders. They cleared fields, planted crops, chopped wood, and prepared freshly killed deer for consumption. The men also made tools and weapons, built canoes, sewed moccasins, and made drums. They built their homes and the tribal buildings.

Women were responsible for the household work and child care, and for growing, storing, and preparing food. They tanned deer and buffalo hides, and they wove fabric for clothing and blankets.

Because food was abundant in this region, Choctaw women had more time for arts and crafts. They made attractive baskets and pottery as well as decorative beadwork. For the baskets, they wove several different kinds of reed or cane into intricate designs. Mothers taught their daughters how to make fine double-weave baskets. The basket maker first carefully chose pieces of cane, which grew in swampy areas. It took skill to weave the basket

Left: A Choctaw family sits in a snug winter home. Below: Choctaw women were skilled at making beautiful, tightly woven baskets such as these.

9

neatly, from bottom to top, in one of the classic Choctaw patterns.

Pottery was also artfully shaped and decorated. Women took clay from the red earth of the region and made it into objects ranging in size from small figures to containers that held several gallons of water. Each new generation of Choctaw women learned to decorate pottery with ancient patterns and markings. Out of berries and wild roots they made dyes for coloring pottery and baskets as well as clothing.

Choctaw children were raised in a loving but careful manner. They had chores to perform, such as collecting water and firewood and gathering nuts and berries. Girls learned from mothers and older sisters how to do women's jobs. Men, mainly their mother's brothers, taught the boys to hunt, fish, and become good warriors.

A woman is splitting cane, which is then woven into a basket.

A child's outdoor chores might require him or her to walk several miles a day. Children were warned against being selfish or lazy. They were told about tiny spirits who came to steal small children who were naughty or did not finish their chores.

Elderly members of the tribe were respected, and they held important positions in the tribe. The oldest man in the village sometimes presented the bride at a marriage ceremony.

The Choctaw viewed marriage as a serious duty, and most couples stayed together for life. Young people chose their own partners. After a simple marriage ceremony, the couple's families exchanged gifts, which often included food and fur robes. A feast and dancing might mark the occasion. Some couples built their own homes, while others went to live with one set of parents.

Food

Their rich land provided the Choctaw with many kinds of food. They caught fish from the rivers and lakes. Meat came from deer, bear, and other game, and from smaller animals—rabbits, otters, squirrels, beavers, and raccoons. The Choctaw also ate wild turkey, pigeons, and other birds.

The fertile soil and warm climate, along with enough rain, allowed the Choctaw to raise many different crops. In addition to corn, they grew beans, squash, white and sweet potatoes, peas, onions, cabbages, melons, pumpkins, and sunflowers. The tribe also grew small amounts of tobacco. Many fruits grew wild, including strawberries, huckleberries, grapes, and crabapples.

At planting time, women and men prepared the fields. Women and children did most of the day-to-day farming. During harvest time, everyone worked together to cut and gather the crops. Special dances, feasts, and games marked the corn harvest each year because corn was such an important staple. Much of the harvested food was placed in community storehouses for winter. When game was scarce, the Choctaw depended on the corn, other vegetables, fruits, meat, and fish that they dried and stored.

Corn was eaten roasted, boiled, or stewed with meats and other vegetables. It was also ground into cornmeal to make various breads and cakes. To make cornmeal, women placed the kernels in the bowl of a slightly hollowed-out log and pounded the corn into meal. Or they ground the corn in a stone mortar—a hollowed-out stone—using a pestle—a club-shaped grinding tool. To make one popular corn dish, women pounded dried kernels with a stick to loosen the outer layers. This left hominy, the soft, inner portion. Hominy was soaked for about eight hours, then cooked in seasoned broth.

Choctaw women prepared vegetables and fruits in different ways, often flavored with herbs, spices, and seeds. Soups were made from combinations of vegetables and, sometimes, meat.

The Choctaw sweetened their food with honey or with maple sugar, made from the sap of the maple tree. Cooking oil, which came from sunflower seeds or from the fat of bear meat, was stored in jars.

The women are grinding corn into cornmeal and boiling corn to make hominy.

12

Hunting and Fishing

Hunting was a vital skill for Choctaw men, and good hunters were much admired. Men used bows and arrows to hunt deer—their main prey—and other large game. They made animal traps out of sticks, flexible tree limbs, and strong twine. A throwing stick called an *iti isth nipa*, was sometimes used to kill rabbits.

Many kinds of fish swam in the rivers, streams, and in the ocean water along the southeast coast. To catch them, the Choctaw used spears, nets, fish traps fashioned from cane, and special barb-pointed arrows attached to lengths of string. Turtles were also caught, cooked, and eaten.

Blowguns were another important weapon for killing animals. To make and use a blowgun well took practice. A Choctaw blowgun, called an *uski thompa*, measured 6 to 8 feet long. It was made from a hollow piece of swamp cane—a plant with a woody stem—that had been hardened with fire. Sharp lengths of twisted cane were shaped into darts, or *shumatti*. By blowing the darts through the gun, a hunter could hit animals at distances of up to 30 feet.

Pairs of Choctaw men often hunted with blowguns at night. One got ready to blow the gun. The other held up a lighted torch to momentarily blind the rabbit or other prey. By age eight, a boy was expected to be able to kill small animals with a blowgun.

Blowguns enabled hunters to hit animals as far away as 30 feet.

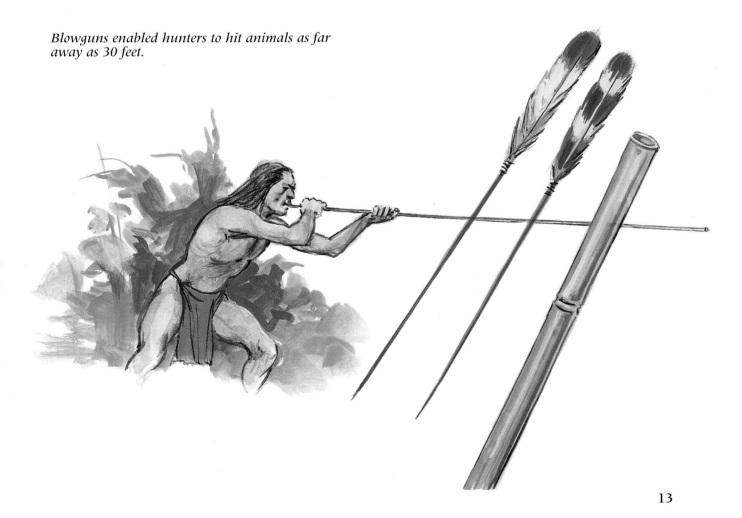

Men used a number of devices for catching fish, including the spears shown here.

Clothing

Choctaw women took pride in making attractive garments that fit well, and men made fine moccasins. Deerskin hides were used for most clothing. In hot weather, people needed few clothes. Men wore a breechcloth—a piece of animal skin tied around the waist and hips. In colder weather, they added leggings and deerskin shirts. Women wore skirts made from plant fibers, deerskin, and eventually from woven cloth. They draped scarves made from plant leaves or cloth around their necks and upper bodies.

It was customary for Choctaw men to have flattened foreheads. As infants, they were strapped to cradle boards that pressed against their foreheads as the bones grew. Choctaw men were also known for their long hair. When a young man reached adulthood, he let his hair grow to show his new status. Men also wore distinctive, round-shaped hats.

Women styled their long hair with combs made from shell, bone, antler, or copper. They adorned their hairdos with beaded ornaments or flowers.

Tattoos were popular. The tattoo designs showed a person's age and rank in the tribe. Young men received special tattoos when they reached adulthood or became warriors. Some Choctaw men pierced their nostrils and wore ornaments made from bear claws. They learned to apply body paint in colors of red, white, and black. When preparing to go to war, men painted their faces with the designs that were used by their clans.

Feathers from eagles and other birds were worn on the head. Important

A man and woman are dressed in traditional Choctaw clothing.

16

A collar made of dyed horsehair was worn as a decorative accessory.

Choctaw men wore fancy headdresses with special feathers that showed their achievements. Shells and bones were made into necklaces, bracelets, and earrings. Both men and women wore jewelry.

Travel

The Choctaw travelled by land over well-worn paths and trails. They marked their trails by painting symbols on trees and rocks or shaping mounds of earth along the trail. One important trail was the Natchez Trace, which went through Mississippi and Tennessee.

Water was the major means for traveling longer distances in the Southeast. The Choctaw paddled their canoes along the rivers and down to the coast, where they traded goods with other Native Americans. Men built dugout canoes from large trees. They burned out the inside, then used stone scrapers and clamshells to carve out an opening the right size and shape. A large canoe might hold twelve to fifteen people. Rafts made of cane were used for transportation in swamp areas.

Games

Games were an important part of Choctaw life. Besides being fun to play, games built the physical strength, coordination, and energy needed by male hunters and warriors. Girls strived to become strong and healthy for motherhood and for the demanding chores that they performed.

The Choctaw played a form of stick-ball, called *toli*, which was also played by northeastern tribes. Eventually, it became known as lacrosse. The game required two teams. Each one might have 100 or more men. The teams opposed each other on a field that was about 500 feet long.

17

A player held a wooden stick with a woven net at the end, which he used to move a ball across a long field. The ball, made of deerskin stuffed with hairs, was about the size of a modern golf ball. Players tried to catch the ball in the net at the end of the stick and throw it between the home goal posts.

Before playing *toli*, the Choctaw recited special prayers. Medicine men moved along the field during the game, asking the spirits to help their team. To get power from the Sun, they held pieces of glass that reflected its rays onto the players' bodies.

Crowds of cheering spectators watched this fast-paced, difficult game. They were eager to see their team win, and they sometimes placed bets on the game's outcome, risking their household goods, clothing, and even horses.

The Choctaw also played *toli* against teams from other tribes, such as the Creek. The best teams in the region then played against each other to determine the regional champions. Sometimes a game was more than a friendly athletic competition. For example, *toli* was played to settle disputes over land.

Another popular game, *chunkey*, was played in a yard or outdoor court. Two players threw long, pointed poles at a smooth, round stone as it rolled along the ground. The winner was the player whose pole landed closest to the ball when it finally stopped. The stone ball used for *chunkey* was treasured by the village, and it was used for generations.

The Choctaw played toli—*an early version of lacrosse—against other Native American tribes.*

Women and men alike played dice games using kernels of dried corn or fruit seeds that were charred on one side. Children also played dice games. They enjoyed simple toys made from common objects. Boys shot small-sized sets of bows and arrows, and girls "mothered" cornhusk dolls.

Political and Social Organization

Choctaw towns governed themselves. Each one elected a town chief and a war chief. When there was a war, groups of towns united so that thousands of people could fight their enemies together.

The town chiefs formed the tribe's national council. The council met once or twice a year to make important decisions affecting the tribe and to make new laws. Towns were free to express disagreement about laws made by the national council.

By the 1400s, there were about sixty or seventy Choctaw towns, grouped into three districts—southern, western, and eastern. Most of the towns and the Choctaw capital of Koweh Chito were in the eastern district. By the 1700s, a head chief lived at the capital. The role of head chief may not have existed until Europeans began coming to Choctaw country. They probably urged the tribe to name a single leader with whom they could deal directly.

Like many Native Americans, the Choctaw chose their leaders, rather than passing these positions from parent to child. Leaders were men who had qualities the Choctaw valued.

They chose men with courage who had the ability to work well with others. The Choctaw also valued good speakers. One important man in the tribe worked both with the political leaders and priests. He was the *yatika*, which meant "long-talker," a person who spoke for the tribe at special events.

Within their villages, the Choctaw belonged to extended families called clans. Each one was made up of several groups of families. A person's ancestry was traced through the mother. A Choctaw was a member of his or her mother's clan. Larger groups within the tribe, called "moieties," were made up of a number of clans.

Clan names came from animals, such as the Panther, Bird, and Bear clans. Every clan had its rules and customs, passed from one generation to the next. The Choctaw worshipped spirits connected with their clans and sang special songs. People were not allowed to marry within their own clan. Good manners required younger clan members to show hospitality to elderly members, who were treated as honored guests.

Under Choctaw laws, a person could be put to death for some offenses, such as murder (which was rare) or for marrying someone from the same clan. Town councils tried to resolve disagreements between individuals—for example, when someone damaged another's property.

The Choctaw believed in taking revenge for wrongdoing. If a murder was committed, a member of the victim's clan would kill the murderer, or if that was not possible, a member of the murderer's clan might be killed instead.

The most common punishment was shaming. Many people who broke the law became social outcasts, mocked by their fellow tribal members or sent away. Men who were not brave in battle were scorned, too. Women did not want to marry someone who had been labelled a coward.

The Choctaw sometimes went to war with one of their neighbors in the Southeast. Men usually fought to protect their lands, homes, and villages. At times, they went to war for revenge or out of anger toward old enemies. As warriors, men could show their courage, skills, and physical strength—traits that were highly valued.

A war usually started at night or at sunrise. During the night, a group consisting of twenty to forty warriors quietly approached the enemy village. The warriors were careful to cover any tracks they left on the ground with leaves or dirt. They walked in single file. One man walked behind another, stepping into his tracks. The leader carried a medicine bundle containing holy objects meant to bring victory.

After they arrived at the enemy village, the warriors divided into smaller groups and surrounded the area. Weapons used for fighting people at close range included clubs, lances, darts, tomahawks, and bows and arrows. Some war captives were taken home as slaves. Captives were sometimes killed in public.

The Choctaw had to be clever to avoid being attacked by others. Native Americans were skilled at detecting campfires from far away and spotting tracks on the ground. Not only could they identify different types of tracks, they could tell how long ago the owners of the tracks had passed by.

A man paints another man's face with body paint in preparation for war.

Religious Life

Spirituality was part of daily life for the Choctaw, just as it was for other Native Americans. The natural world and humans were viewed as parts of the same whole, which must stay in balance. Special religious ceremonies marked important events. Children learned their religious traditions and history through stories told by older members of the tribe.

For the Choctaw, the Sun was the major spiritual being. They also believed that people, animals, and all of nature had spirits that should be respected. The Choctaw performed special chants or songs when hunting. Hunters might first apologize before killing an animal, and they did not kill more than the people needed for food.

A person's spirit was viewed as sacred. The Choctaw thought dreams were the spirit's nighttime activities. With the help of priests and medicine makers, people tried to figure out what their dreams might mean.

These holy men (and occasionally, women) were highly respected by the Choctaw. They were thought to have the powers of healing and of seeing into the future.

Medicine makers were chosen from among the Choctaw's priests. They learned the chants and ceremonies performed for the sick. These healers also knew of special charms and herbs for treating illnesses, and they kept medicine bundles. These pouches of animal hide contained sacred objects for healing and for tribal ceremonies. Sacred objects included pipes, rattles, and medicine tubes. The bundles were hidden when not in use.

The Choctaw kept charms and objects to give themselves special powers. Some were very old. They might be made of stone, gems, shells, feathers, animal teeth, or bone. Some were strung into necklaces or worn around the neck on a length of animal string.

Surrounded by many gifts from nature, such as the crops they grew and the deer they hunted, the Choctaw believed they were especially blessed by the spirits. Many ceremonies enabled people to give thanks. Corn was regarded as a great gift from the spirits. For eight days at harvest time, the Choctaw held a Green Corn Festival to give thanks for this life-giving crop. People fasted and then celebrated the arrival of the first corn of the season. The vegetable harvest was a time of renewal and fresh starts. People cleaned their homes and discarded broken pottery. New fires were started in the village altar, which holy men kept burning year-round. People settled old quarrels.

The Choctaw performed special dances, with complex steps, to celebrate the harvest. They also danced at festivals, religious ceremonies, and at weddings. Warriors performed dances before going to war.

The Eagle Dance was performed by twelve to sixteen men, who took turns dancing in groups of four. They wore body paint made from white clay. Each dancer wore an eagle feather in his hair and held the tail of an eagle.

Choctaw men wearing white body paint and eagle feathers perform the Eagle Dance. They are dancing around spears that are stuck in the ground.

The men danced to the beat of a drum, circling around spears that were jabbed into the ground.

Spirituality was an important part of the rituals surrounding death, as it was throughout life. After death, the Choctaw believed they would join their ancestors in the afterlife. Ceremonies were held for the dead. If the dead person was an important member of the tribe, speeches were made in his or her honor by the *yatika*, the leading speaker.

Before burial, the body was placed on a scaffold. A man or woman called a "bone picker" removed the skin from the bones, which were put in special baskets. The Choctaw believed that the bones of their ancestors were sacred. Poles were set up around new graves. On them, people hung wreaths and other things that would help the dead person's spirit on its journey to the afterlife.

There was intense mourning for the dead, especially when important warriors died. Each year, family members took time out to mourn for all those who had passed away. To mark this mourning period, people fasted and covered their heads.

European Contact

Whites first reached the area that is now southeastern United States in 1539. In that year, Spanish explorers led by Hernando De Soto arrived, looking for gold and silver. They found no such treasures, however. Fighting broke out between Native Americans and the disappointed Spaniards. In 1540, De Soto's troops burned a Choctaw city, killing 1,500 people.

The next group of whites to reach this region were the French, who came at the end of the 1600s. The French settlers established the colony of Louisiana on the Mississippi River. To win Choctaw support for their colony, they traded metal tools, wool blankets, and other goods for animal skins and furs. The Choctaw were curious to know these whites but were also suspicious as a result of their experiences with De Soto's men. By the 1700s, about 20,000 Choctaw lived in the Southeast.

The French settled in what are now New Orleans, Louisiana; Mobile, Alabama; and Biloxi, Mississippi. In 1729, some French traders presented 800 pounds of gifts to 160 Choctaw leaders in east-central Mississippi. These gifts included clothing, blankets, woolen cloth, guns and powder, and hatchets. A feast was prepared for the French, and the Choctaw performed special dances in their honor. That same year, the Choctaw helped the French to defeat a group of Natchez Indians whom they had been fighting for several months.

From the French, the Choctaw adopted some white ways of doing things that changed their lives. They began using new tools and machines, including plows and spinning wheels. They raised cattle, pigs, poultry, and horses. Eventually, they developed a breed that became known as the Choctaw pony. By running trading posts and other businesses, some Choctaw became wealthy. There were marriages between whites and Choctaw, usually between Choctaw women and white traders.

European men came to the Southeast to trade with the Choctaw and other tribes.

Conflicts broke out between the French and English. The English defeated the French in the French and Indian War, which lasted from 1754 to 1763. The Choctaw supported France, but did not fight actively against the English. After the war, the tribe continued to live in Mississippi while England was in control. A few Choctaw villages moved to Louisiana to be near the French.

Native Americans began suffering from problems brought by the increasing numbers of white settlers. The settlers brought diseases that were new to the Choctaw, such as smallpox and measles. The Choctaw lacked the natural ability to fight off these diseases, which only develops when diseases have been around for generations. As a result, thousands died. The Choctaw also came to rely more on tools and other goods brought by the traders and were less independent.

By the late 1700s, the American colonists wanted to free themselves from British control. The Choctaw lived outside the thirteen colonies and did not fight in the Revolutionary War, although both sides sought their support. After the war, the Choctaw signed a treaty with the new U.S. government. The treaty showed the boundaries of Choctaw lands in the Southeast.

Problems soon arose. European settlers were drawn to the lush, green Southeast with its fine soil. The Louisiana Purchase, signed by President Thomas Jefferson in 1803, enabled the United States to claim the land between the Mississippi River and the Rocky Mountains. Thousands more whites moved onto Choctaw lands in Mississippi. They wanted more land, and many of them urged the government to force the Choctaw and other Native American tribes to leave. They wanted to settle where they wished without any interference.

By 1800, the Choctaw lost a lot of land, including some of their hunting grounds. Often, the people did not have enough food; nor could they find enough animals in their reduced territory to obtain furs to trade for other things they needed.

In 1805, the U.S. government forced the Choctaw to sign a treaty that stated they were giving up 4 million acres of their ancestral lands. With that, the tribe hoped that the government would leave it alone. As the years passed, however, whites demanded more land. They insisted that the Choctaw sign more treaties, each time promising this concession would be the last. Little by little, the Choctaw were forced off their land. The same concessions were demanded of other tribes, such as the Cherokee of Georgia.

The Choctaw expected better treatment from the Americans. They had sided with them against various enemies. With the Cherokee, the Choctaw helped General Andrew Jackson defeat the Creek Indians in 1813. More than 700 Choctaw warriors, led by their respected leader, Pushmataha, took part in this war. They also helped Jackson's troops to defeat the British in the War of 1812.

During the 1820s, Choctaw lands were reduced even more. The Indian Removal Act became law in 1830. Under this act, the president of the United States had the right to give Native American tribes land in Indian

Territory (later Oklahoma) in exchange for their eastern homelands.

Like other southeastern tribes, the Choctaw did not want to move. For generations, they had built homes, farms, communities, and religious sites on these lands. The rocks, streams, and forests were dear to them, as were the grave sites of their ancestors.

As the southeastern tribes resisted, the government pushed harder to get them out. New laws stripped them of their lands and their rights. Mississippi passed a law that made tribal governments illegal, which meant the Choctaw could not honor their own laws. The U.S. intended to force all the Native Americans west.

The Choctaw lost all hope of keeping their beautiful lands. The United States had a large, well-equipped army. In 1830, under great pressure from U.S. officials, Choctaw leaders signed the Treaty of Dancing Rabbit Creek. According to the agreement, the Choctaw would give up their remaining land—over 10 million acres—and go to a piece of land that had been set aside for them in the Arkansas territory.

The Choctaw were the first of the Five Nations to leave for the West. The Five Nations' sad journey to Indian Territory became known as the Trail of Tears. In November 1831, about 4,000 Choctaw left their lands and possessions and set out on foot for the West. Other groups of Choctaw followed, along with the Creek, Seminole, Cherokee, and Chickasaw— about 50,000 people in all. It was an unusually cold winter, and the Mississippi River was clogged with ice. After crossing the river, the Choctaw then had to cross the snow-covered Great Arkansas Swamp. They wore thin clothing, and some had no shoes. Many died of cold and hunger, or from sickness.

In the West, the Choctaw were sent to an area around Fort Towson. Harsh conditions awaited them in this unfamiliar region with a drier climate than they had known before. With no crops or money, they often went hungry. Although traders were paid by the U.S. government to bring food to the tribes, these traders often brought poor-quality food or none at all. Smallpox, cholera, dysentery, and other diseases killed thousands of Native Americans. Poor nutrition weakened people, leaving them even less able to fight off disease.

About 1,000 Choctaw refused to leave Mississippi. Instead they moved to swampy areas in the eastern part of the state, where they hoped they would not be noticed. They lived as outsiders in a region they had once proudly called home, and they hid to avoid being arrested by government officials.

When the Chickasaw arrived in Indian Territory in the fall of 1837, the U.S. government grouped them with the Choctaw as one tribe. In 1855 a new treaty finally recognized the two groups as separate.

The Choctaw set up a tribal government of their own and wrote a constitution that established the laws for members of the tribe. Like other Native Americans from the Southeast, the Choctaw overcame many problems, and they succeeded in building a strong, well-organized government.

The Choctaw Today

In the years that followed, the U.S. government often broke its promises to the Choctaw. Changing government policies toward Native Americans continued to affect them. During the late 1800s, the government urged Native Americans to assimilate—to adopt the customs of the white majority culture. The government forced some Native American children to attend boarding schools and adopt the Christian religion.

The Curtis Act, passed in 1898, caused further problems. This act said that individual Native Americans in Indian Territory would receive their own parcels of land. The rest was to be sold. The act meant the loss of more land for the Choctaw, and it ended tribal ownership of land. In 1906, a law was passed prohibiting tribal governments.

In 1907, Indian Territory became the state of Oklahoma. Around the same time, oil was found in the state. More white settlers came to search for this valuable natural resource. The Choctaw and other tribes in Oklahoma continued to suffer from poverty, poor health care, and the lack of jobs and education. They now made up only about 6 percent of the state's population.

In 1917, a flu epidemic raged throughout the world. Many of the Choctaw who had remained in Mississippi became sick and died. Concerned citizens urged the U.S. government to help the Mississippi Choctaw. The government gave them some land around their villages in the southeastern part of the state and built a few schools there.

Life was still hard. The Mississippi Choctaw had trouble finding decent jobs and were often insulted and mistreated by whites in their communities. Signs of hope came during the 1960s. For years, African Americans had been working hard to end racial discrimination. The civil rights movement swept across America and led to the passage of important laws, such as the Civil Rights Act of 1964. This law made it illegal to keep people out of jobs, housing, or education because of their race or religion. The law helped Native Americans who were being treated unfairly.

During these years, the U.S. government changed its attitude toward Native Americans. More people supported their right to follow their own ways and religions. There was a growing interest in traditional songs, dances, crafts, and religious customs. In the 1960s, more than 40,000 Choctaw lived on their reservation, located in southeastern Oklahoma. About 4,000 lived in Mississippi.

In 1975, Congress passed the Indian Self-Determination Act. It set up ways for tribes to rule themselves with financial help from the government. With these funds, tribes could build schools and other buildings and set up more businesses in their communities.

The Mississippi Band of Choctaw Indians worked hard for economic success. In 1979, Chief Philip Martin led the group in setting up a business owned and run by the tribe. This was the first of five industrial plants that the Choctaw developed, providing jobs

Although many of the Choctaw went on the long, sad journey to the West, known as the Trail of Tears, some remained in Mississippi.

This woman is an herbalist. She knows which herbs and other plants have healing powers.

for large numbers of employees. The tribe manufactures greeting cards, assembles telephones, and prints direct-mail advertisements.

Like all Native Americans, the Choctaw have had to find ways to preserve their unique heritage while living and working in the modern world. They have worked hard to improve their educational and job opportunities and to bring better health care to the Oklahoma reservation and to Mississippi, where many Choctaw live. A number of them also live in towns and cities throughout the nation.

To keep their old ways alive, the Choctaw in both Oklahoma and Mississippi have taught young people the tribe's language and customs. Choctaw men and boys living both in Oklahoma and Mississippi still play *toli*. Spectators are awed by the skill and speed of these athletes. The Choctaw hold annual fairs at which traditional dances and songs are performed. Old people who know how to weave baskets and make pottery have taught their crafts to younger generations. As a result, the unique Choctaw heritage lives on.

Chronology

1540   Spanish explorers led by Hernando De Soto are the first Europeans to make contact with the Choctaw.

1699   French colonists establish Louisiana.

1729   French traders meet with 160 Choctaw leaders. They offer 800 pounds of gifts and ask the Choctaw to support their war against the Natchez tribe.

1781   The Choctaw sign a treaty with the newly formed United States that defines the boundaries of the Choctaw's lands.

1803   Under the Louisiana Purchase, the U.S. government agrees to buy the Louisiana Territory from France. The United States claims all lands between the Mississippi River and the Rocky Mountains.

1805   The U.S. government forces the Choctaw to sign a treaty giving up 4 million acres of land.

1830   Under President Andrew Jackson, the U.S. Congress passes the Indian Removal Act.
Choctaw leaders sign the Treaty of Dancing Rabbit Creek on September 27, giving up their remaining 10,423,130 acres in Mississippi.

1830–1833   The Choctaw are the first of the southeastern tribes to be removed to Indian Territory.
Of the 3,000 Choctaw who migrate west, 600 die of disease or cold during the trip or soon after arrival. About 1,000 Choctaw stay behind, hiding in swampy areas.

1855   U.S. officials recognize the Choctaw and Chickasaw as two distinct tribes.

1898   Congress passes the Curtis Act, which results in the loss of more Choctaw lands in Indian Territory.

1906   Congress passes a law making tribal governments illegal.

1907   Oklahoma, formerly called Indian Territory, becomes a state.

1917   The suffering of the Mississippi Choctaw during a flu epidemic brings them to the attention of concerned Americans.

1964   Congress passes the Civil Rights Act, which bans discrimination in jobs, education, and housing on the basis of race, religion, or nationality.

1975   Congress passes the Indian Self-Determination Act, allowing tribes to develop their own systems of government.

1979   Under Chief Philip Martin, the Mississippi Choctaw open the first of five industrial plants owned and run by the tribe.

INDEX

Acknowledgments and Photo Credits
Cover and all artwork by Richard Smolinski.
Photographs on pages 9 and 17: ©Hillel Burger/Peabody Museum, Harvard University; pages 17 and 30: ©Dick Durrance/National Geographic Society Image Collection.
Map by Blackbirch Graphics, Inc.